CIVIL AIRCRAFT OF THE WORLD

Hiroshi Seo

First published in Japan in 1979 by
Yama-Kei Publishers Co Ltd, Tokyo

Photographs © Hiroshi Seo, 1979

Text © Jane's Publishing Co Ltd, 1981

First published in Great Britain in 1981 by
Jane's Publishing Company Ltd
238 City Road, London EC1V 2PU

ISBN 0 7106 0102 6

Printed in Japan

JANE'S LONDON · SYDNEY

Contents

Piston-Engined Airliners

Front Cover: Boeing 747SR (Japan Air Lines)
Rear Cover: Cockpit of Concorde (Air France)

BAe/Aérospatiale Concorde

The birth certificate for Concorde was a 1962 Anglo-French agreement covering the joint development of a supersonic transport (SST). Seven years later, after momentous design and development efforts at the frontiers of high technology, the French prototype, 001, took to the air on March 2, 1969. The British prototype, 002, followed on April 9.

The ogival delta wing is efficient across a very wide speed band, although the necessarily slim fuselage can seat only four abreast. The variable-geometry nose and visor are "drooped" for take-off and landing and raised for supersonic flight. Four afterburning turbojets propel Concorde to above Mach 2 at cruising altitudes of up to 18,288 m (60,000 ft), though at the expense of excessive noise and sonic boom effects.

After extensive flight testing and to a background of protests and controversy, British Airways and Air France began scheduled services on May 24, 1976. The route network grew substantially but the programme took a knock when Braniff and Singapore Airlines withdrew from operating their sectors. A question mark now hangs over the operating economics advanced by the original Concorde protagonists. The development programme grossly overran in time and money, and this brave venture into civil supersonic transport seems unlikely to redeem itself in airline service. Production ended in April 1979 after 16 Concordes and four prototypes had been built. *Span:* 25.55 m (83 ft 10 in) *Length:* 62.1 m (203 ft 9 in) *Max take-off weight:* 185,065 kg (407,994 lb) *Powerplant:* 4 × Rolls-Royce/Snecma Olympus afterburning turbojets, each 17,260 kg (38,050 lb) st *Max cruising speed:* Mach 2.04 *Range:* 6,228 km (3,870 miles) *Accommodation:* 144 passengers, 3 crew

Left: Concorde G-N94AA of British Airways at Heathrow. Above: Cockpit (left) and flight engineer's position (right). Right: Air France Concorde F-BTSC of Air France at Charles de Gaulle. Below right: Visor down and nose drooped on a BA/Singapore Airlines Concorde (Left: 105mm KR f5.6 + ⅓ 1/500)

Tupolev Tu-144

The Tu-144 was the first supersonic airliner in the world to fly and the first to enter service, beating Concorde into the air by two months. But since its first flight in 1968 the aircraft has been beset by technical problems and is no longer in airline service.

During the flight-test programme the need for a major redesign became apparent and the aircraft reappeared in 1973 in slightly enlarged form and with repositioned engine nacelles and retractable canard foreplanes to improve low-speed handling. However, a disastrous crash at the 1973 Paris Show further retarded development.

Four reheated turbofans gave the Tu-144 a cruising speed of Mach 2.35, faster than Concorde, but lack of range limited the type's commercial service to flights between Moscow and Alma Ata. Passenger services began in 1977 but these were suspended in 1978 after further technical and fuel-consumption problems. *Span:* 28.8 m (94 ft 6 in) *Length:* 65.7 m (215 ft 6½ in) *Max take-off weight:* 180,000 kg (396,825 lb) *Powerplant:* 4 × Kuznetsov NK-144 afterburning turbofans, each 20,000 kg (44,092 lb) st *Max cruising speed:* Mach 2.35 *Range:* 6,500 km (4,039 miles) *Accommodation:* 140 passengers, 3 crew

Tupolev Tu-144 CCCP-77110 in Aeroflot colours at the 1977 Paris Show (Left: 300mm KR f5.6 + ⅔ 1/500. Above: 200mm KR f5.6 + ⅔ 1/500. Right above: 200mm KR f5.6 + ⅔ 1/500. Below: 105mm KR f5.6 1/250)

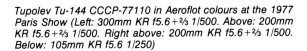

Boeing 747

The appearance in airline service of Boeing's mighty "Jumbo" represented a real leap forward in airliner technology and engendered a second revolution in air travel. With passenger capacity almost three times that of the largest 707, the 747 forced Boeing to solve new problems of airframe and systems design.

Powered by the new generation of big turbofan engines, the first 747 flew in February 1969. In January 1970 the type entered service with Pan Am on the North Atlantic, ushering in the age of wide-body mass air travel. The 747's unique spaciousness and attractive operating economics quickly endeared it to passengers and operators alike.

The initial version was the -100, followed by the -200 with increased fuel capacity and longer range. The latter was offered with different powerplants, including the Rolls-Royce RB.211, and as the all-cargo -200F or convertible passenger/cargo -200CF. The 747SP with a shorter fuselage is designed for extreme long-range operations and the 747SR for economic operations over short distances. (**747-200B**) *Span:* 59.6 m (195 ft 8 in) *Length:* 70.51 m (231 ft 4 in) *Max take-off weight:* 322,050 kg (710,000 lb) *Powerplant:* 4 × JT9D, CF6 or RR RB.211 turbofans, each 22,680–24,040 kg (50–53,000 lb) st *Max cruising speed:* 967 km/h (601 mph) *Range:* 8,330 km (5,180 miles) *Accommodation:* 442 passengers, 2/3 crew

Left: JAL Boeing 747-200B JA8105. Above: 747SR cockpit. Right: 747-100 of United Airlines lands at Los Angeles with its triple-slotted trailing-edge flaps fully deployed. Below right: JAL 747-200F JA8144 (Left: 105 mm KR f5.6+⅔ 1/500. Above: 28 mm KR Speedlight f5.6 1/60. Right above: 200 mm KM f5.6 1/250. Below: 50 mm KR f8 1/250)

Boeing 747SP ZS-SPB Outeniqua *of South African Airways lands at Athens (105 mm KM f5.6 + ⅓ 1/250)*

Boeing 747SP

The Boeing 747SP (Special Performance), which first flew in 1973, was a complete structural re-design aimed at optimum long-range performance. The fuselage was shortened by 14.2 m (47 ft), weight reduced, some systems simplified and the tail increased in size. Passenger accommodation was reduced to 281 but the range exceeds 9,000 km (5,400 miles), allowing non-stop flights between New York and Tokyo, for example. SP customers include Iranair, Pan Am, South African Airways and Syrianair.

Boeing 747SR
The 747SR is a high-density variant of the basic 747 designed for short-haul services and incorporating structural changes made necessary by high take-off and

All Nippon Airways 747SR JA8136 (200 mm KM f5.6 + ⅓ 1/250)

landing cycles. The 14 examples built are all operated by JAL and Air Nippon, serving on domestic routes and seating a record 500 passengers.

Ilyushin Il-86

The Soviet Union's first wide-bodied jet, the Il-86, NATO code-named *Camber*, was first reported in 1971 as a medium-range transport capable of carrying over 200 passengers. By 1976 the original proposal with four rear-mounted turbofans and a T-tail had been dropped and the aircraft had grown in size. The main features of this extensive redesign were under-wing pylon-mounted engines and a tail located at the rear of the fuselage. An extra landing leg under the centre fuselage carries a four-wheel bogie to further distribute the weight of this large aircraft, which weighs only slightly less than the Lockheed TriStar.

The maiden flight of the Il-86 was in December 1976 and the West got its first look at the USSR's first wide-body at the Paris Show in late spring 1977 when prototype 86000 flew into Le Bourget.

The Il-86 features a double-deck fuselage with twin aisles and three ranks of three-abreast seating on the upper deck. The lower deck is used for freight and baggage. In contrast to Western practice, passengers board at the lower deck, stow their baggage and coats, and climb one of three stairways into the passenger compartment. Integral airstairs and this self-help system give Aeroflot flexibility at poorly equipped airports.

The Il-86 has an exceptionally sturdy airframe which is reported to be capable of 40,000 flying hours. Its powerplant and aerodynamics are outmoded, however, and the high specific fuel consumption of its Kuznetsov turbofans imposes a high weight penalty in extra fuel. A long-range intercontinental version would need redesigned wings of increased span and would have to be powered by high-bypass-ratio turbofans such as the Rolls-Royce RB.211 or General Electric CF.6. (**Il-86**) *Span:* 48.06 m (157 ft 8 in) *Length:* 59.54 m (195 ft 4 in) *Max take-off weight:* 206,000 kg (455,000 lb) *Powerplant:* 4 × Kuznetsov NK-86 turbofans 13,000 kg (26,660 lb) st *Max speed:* 950 km/h (590 mph) *Range:* 3,600 km (2,235 miles) *Accommodation:* 350 passengers, 3/4 crew

Prototype Il-86 CCCP-86000 seen at the 1979 Paris Show in Aeroflot colours. The integral airstairs (top right) are important for operations from poorly equipped airports (Left: 300 mm KR f5.6+⅓ 1/500, Right top: 28 mm KM f5.6 1/250. Below: 105 mm KM f5.6 1/250)

Ilyushin Il-76T

A high-performance heavy-lifter and strategic transport, the Il-76, NATO code-named *Candid*, was developed in response to a military requirement for an aircraft able to carry a load of 40,000 kg over 5,000 km in under six hours. The aircraft has exceptional short- and rough-field performance and on-board auxiliary power.

Il-76T CCCP-76500 of Aeroflot seen at Paris in 1979. (200 mm KR f5.6 + ⅓ 1/500)

(Il-76T) *Span:* 50.5 m (165 ft 8 in) *Length:* 46.59 m (152 ft 10¼ in) *Max take-off weight:* 170,000 kg (374,780 lb) *Powerplant:* 4 × Soloviev D-30KP turbofans (each 12,000 kg (26,455 lb) st *Max cruising speed:* up to 800 km/h (497 mph) *Range:* 5,000 km (3,100 miles) *Accommodation:* 40,000 kg (88,183 lb) freight, 3 crew

Delta Airlines Lockheed L-1011 TriStar N714DA at Miami Airport (50 mm KM f4 1/500)

Lockheed L-1011 TriStar

Incorporating advanced systems engineering and powered by advanced-technology Rolls-Royce RB.211 turbofans, Lockheed's venture into the wide-body field brought the company to the brink of commercial disaster in the early 1970s when development delays let the rival Douglas DC-10 capture much of the US and international market for a medium-range trijet. The TriStar recovered strongly, however, and since its first flight in 1970 has been developed through several variants. Orders stand at over 200 examples

L-1011 TriStar

The original L-1011-1 was designed for short/medium-haul operations. 1973 saw the introduction of the -100 with more fuel and powered by RB.211-22B turbofans with improved take-off rating. The -200 has a redesigned interior with a repositioned galley, and an additional centre-section fuel tank. The -500, with a slightly shortened fuselage, incorporates active ailerons, which automatically relieve the wings of local gust stresses, allowing greater span and thus increased cruising range. (**L-1011-500**) *Span:* 47.34 m (155 ft 4 in) *Length:* 50.05 m (164 ft 2½ in) *Max take-off weight:* 224,980 kg (496,000 lb) *Powerplant:* 3 × RB.211-524B turbofans, each 22,680 kg (50,000 lb) st *Max cruising speed:* 973 km/h (605 mph) *Range:* 9,653 km (5,998 miles) *Accommodation:* 300 passengers, 3 crew

Left: All Nippon Airways L-1011-1 JA8518. Below left: Gulf Air L-1011-100 A40-TX. Above: Cockpit of an L-1011-1. Right: L-1011-500 registered N48354 for tests and operated by British Airways as G-BFCA (Left top: 600 mm KR f5.6 + ⅓ 1/500. Below: 105 mm KR f8 1/500. Above: 28 mm KR S.I. f5.6 1/60. Right: 200 mm KM f4 + ½ 1/500)

McDonnell Douglas DC-10-10
Second of the wide-bodies, the DC-10 got into the air just weeks before its Lockheed rival in 1970, and first went into airline service with American Airlines in August 1971. The initial model was the DC-10-10 powered by three GE CF6-D1 turbofans and seating up to 345 passengers. It met the needs of US domestic operators looking for

American Airlines DC-10-10 N126AA landing at Los Angeles (200 mm KR f5.6 + ⅔ 1/500)

large capacity on internal trunk routes of between 480 to 5,795 km (300 to 3,600 miles). Orders were substantial and in spite of some initial operating problems McDonnell Douglas embarked on an ambitious development programme.

DC-10-30 XA-DUG of Aeromexico (200 mm KR f5.6 + ⅔ 1/500)

McDonnell Douglas DC-10-30
The -30 is a long-range intercontinental version with wing span increased by 3.05 m (10 ft) and an additional twin-wheel undercarriage unit below the centre fuselage to carry the increased weight. The -30 started service with Swissair on the North Atlantic in 1972 and has been the biggest-selling variant. (**DC-10-30**) *Span:* 50.39 m (165 ft 4 in) *Length:* 55.35 m (181 ft 7¾ in) *Max take-off weight:* 251,744 kg (550,000 lb) *Powerplant:* 3 × Pratt & Whitney JT9D-20 turbofans, each 22,000 kg (48,500 lb) st *Max cruising speed:* 956 km/h (594 mph) *Range:* 7,413 km (4,606 miles) *Accommodation:* 345 passengers, 5 crew

McDonnell Douglas DC-10-40
The -40 is a refinement of the -30 long-range version, with Pratt & Whitney JT9D-20 turbofans of greater power and with water injection. The first flight of this model was

DC-10-40s N144US and N155US of Northwest Orient at Tampa, Florida (300 mm KR f5.6 + 1/500) in February 1972 and scheduled operations were begun by Northwest Orient Airlines later in the year.

Airbus A300

The new generation of very efficient big turbofans which powered the 1970 generation of US wide-bodies was applied in Europe to a large-capacity "airbus" designed for maximum economy over short-haul routes. The A300 was designed by the Airbus Industrie consortium, which includes Aérospatiale, MBB, VFW-Fokker,

Airbus A300B-2-300 F-WZEN, which later became LN-RCA of Scandinavian Airlines System (300 mm KR f5.6 + ⅔ 1/500)

CASA and BAe, and the prototype first flew in 1972. Since then development has proceeded very smoothly and the A300 now operates with airlines around the world. A shorter version seating 200 and with a redesigned wing is under development as the A310

21

Airbus A300

Although the A300 is only slightly smaller overall than the wide-bodied US trijets, its operating economics on short-haul routes are markedly better. The 1970s increases in fuel costs have given the A300 a sales boost, and its mix of range and payload has proved very attractive to operators.

The type has also been developed through several versions: the B2K with heavy-duty undercarriage, the B4 with increased fuel and range, and the C4 freight or convertible passenger/freight version. At the customer's request some B4-200s have Pratt & Whitney JT9D engines. By 1980 continued development had led to the use of composite material for some structural parts, and the fitting of advanced cockpit instrumentation. (**A300B2-100**) *Span:* 44.84 m (147 ft 1¼ in) *Length:* 53.75 m (175 ft 9 in) *Max take-off weight:* 142,000 kg (313,055 lb) *Powerplant:* 2 × GE CF6-50C turbofans, each 23,034 kg (51,000 lb) st *Max cruising speed:* 935 km/h (582 mph) *Range:* 1,610 km (1,000 miles) *Accommodation:* 336 passengers, 3 crew

Left: A300B4-100 D-AHLB of Hapag-Lloyd. Above: A300 cockpit. Above right: A300B4-100 HK-202057 of Aerocondor. Below right: Thai Air A300B-4-100 HS-TGL (Left: 300 mm KR f5.6 + ⅔ 1/500 Above: 28 mm Speedlight f5.6 1/60. Right top: 300 mm KR f5.6 + ⅔ 1/500. Below: 200 mm KR f8 1/500)

Douglas DC-8

With its pre-eminence in the field of civil transports established by a successful line of piston-engined airliners from the DC-3 to the DC-7, the Douglas company took up the challenge of the jet engine in the mid 1950s slightly later than the rival Boeing Company. The Douglas DC-8 did however partner Boeing's 707 in ushering in the airline jet age.

The Series 10 first flew in 1958 and Douglas was successful in developing the same basic airframe with alternative power-plants, offering different combinations of payload and range to suit customer needs. The Series 40 featured the advanced Rolls-Royce Conway turbofans, the Series 50 had JT3D turbo-fans, and the Series 54 Jet Trader is a convertible passenger/cargo aircraft.

The stretched DC-8 Series 60 appeared in 1965, its fuselage stretched by 11.18 m (36 ft 8 in) to seat up to 259 passengers.

The Series 62 had less stretch but incorporated a major wing redesign giving greater efficiency over long ranges. The final Series 63 combined the new wing with the long fuselage and was offered in passenger and convertible freight versions.

The Super Sixty series still offer a very competitive balance of payload and range. With long airframe lives and a turbofan re-engining programme they look set to serve for many years to come.

Left: JAL DC-8-61 JA8-59 takes off from Narita. Above: DC-8-62F cockpit. Above right: JAL DC-8-62 JA8052. Below right: Saudia DC-8-63CF N8632, a convertible passenger/cargo aircraft (Left: 105 mm KR f8 1/500. Above: 200 mm KR f5.6 1/60. Right: 200 mm KR f5.6 + ⅓ 1/300. Below: 200 mm KR f5.6 + ⅓ 1/500)

DC-8-62 N1805 of Braniff International in a scheme designed by US painter Alexander Calder (300 mm KR f5.6 + ⅓ 1/500)

Douglas DC-8 Super Sixty

The second-generation DC-8 Super Sixty series proved a convincing commercial success and 262 of all models were built. The Series 62 featured only moderate fuselage stretch but had a new wing, increased fuel tankage and new engine pods and pylons. This variant offers excellent efficiency over very long ranges. (**DC-8**

Super 62) *Span:* 45.23 m (148 ft 5 in) *Length:* 47.08 m (157 ft 5 in) *Length:* 47.08 m (157 ft 5 in) *Max take-off weight:* 151,950 kg (335,000 lb) *Powerplant:* 4 × JT3D-7 turbofans, each 8,618 kg (19,000 lb) st *Max cruising speed:* 933 km/h (580 mph) *Range:* 9,640 km (6,000 miles) *Accommodation:* 189 passengers, 3/5 crew

Boeing 707

The Comet 1 was the first jet airliner to enter service but it was the Boeing 707 that really ushered in the age of jet air travel. The 367-80 (or "Dash Eighty") prototype four-engined flight-refuelling tanker/transport first flew in July 1954 and the USAF placed large orders for the tanker version, the KC-135. Boeing reworked the pro-

Boeing 707-320B HK-2015, in service with Colombian airline Avianca (300 mm KR f5.6 + ⅓ 1/500)

totype with a larger fuselage cross-section and America's first production turbojet airliner went into service with Pan Am in 1958. Since then the Boeing 707 has been developed through several versions, including cargo and mixed passenger/cargo variants.

28

Boeing 707-320/720

The original civil 707-720 of 1958 had only limited range and was ultimately overtaken by the rival Douglas DC-8. But in 1959 Boeing produced the 707 Intercontinental, offered as the -320 with JT4A turbojets and the -420 with Rolls-Royce Conway turbofans, and both capable of much greater range and more payload. The use of the new JT3D turbofan, available from 1960 onwards, on the -320B made the aircraft safer and much quieter, and improvements to the wing aerodynamics further improved operating efficiency. Convertible cargo versions are designated with a C suffix, turbofan-powered models with a B.

Outwardly identical to the -120, the Boeing 720 is in fact a completely different design in terms of weight and structural strength. Designed for operations over intermediate ranges, the 720 first flew in 1959. Some 920 707-720s have been built.
(**Boeing 707-320B**) *Span:* 44.42 m (145 ft 9 in) *Length:* 46.61 m (152 ft 11 in) *Max take-off weight:* 151,315 kg (333,600 lb) *Powerplant:* 4 × Pratt & Whitney JT3D-2 turbofans, each 8,165 (18,000 lb) st *Max cruising speed:* 966 km/h (600 mph) *Range:* 9,915 km (6160 miles) *Accommodation:* 189 passengers, 4 crew

Left: 707-320C 9K-ACM of Kuwait Airways. Short-fuselage 720B N93149 of Western Airlines. Bangladesh Biman 707-320C S2ABN, a convertible cargo/passenger example (Left: 300 mm KR f5.6 + ⅔ 1/500. Right above: 50 mm KR f5.6 + ⅔ 1/500. Below: 300 mm KR f8 1/500)

Il-62 OK-GBH of CSA at Prague Airport (105 mm KM f5.6 1/250)

Ilyushin Il-62

The Il-62, NATO code-named *Classic*, was the Soviet Union's first four-engined long-range airliner. It first flew in 1963, some months after the BAC VC.10, the only other large four-rearjet airliner to be built. Full-scale production began in 1965 and the type entered regular service with Aeroflot in 1967. (**Il-62M**) *Span:* 43.2 m (141 ft 9 in) *Length:* 53.12 m (174 ft 3½ in) *Max take-off weight:* 165,000 kg (363,760 lb) *Powerplant:* 4 × Soloviev D-30KU turbofans, each 11,500 kg (25,353 lb) st *Max cruising speed:* 900 km/h (559 mph) *Range:* 9,600 km (5,965 miles) *Accommodation:* 186 passengers, 5/7 crew

BAC (BAe) VC10 *VC10 Series 1102 9G-ABO, one of the two delivered to Ghana Airways in 1964–65 and still in service, seen at Heathrow in 1979 (50 mm KR f5.6 + ⅔ 1/500)*
Designed by Vickers in response to a BOAC requirement for a long-range airliner with hot-and-high airfield capabilities, the VC10 first flew in 1962, followed by the stretched Super VC10 in 1964. Some 56 were built by BAC over eight years and they have proved tough and reliable in airline and RAF service. (**VC10 Series 1100**)

Span: 42.72 m (140 ft 2 in) *Length:* 48.36 m (158 ft 8 in) *Max take-off weight:* 142,430 kg (314,000 lb) *Powerplant:* 4 × Rolls-Royce Conway turbofans, each 9,240 kg (20,370 lb) st *Max cruising speed:* 914 km/h (550 mph) *Range:* 8,115 km (5,040 miles) *Accommodation:* 151 passengers, 3/5 crew

CV-990 30-5 re-registered as N990AB for use as a flying testbed by Garret AiResearch (50 mm KM f5.6 + ⅓ 1/250)

Convair 990 Coronado

The turbofan-powered Convair 990 Coronado failed to compete successfully with its contemporary rivals, the Boeing 707 and DC-8. The characteristic "speed bump" fairings on the wing trailing edges overcame aerodynamic problems, but the programme proved a commercial disaster for Convair, losing over $450 million.

(CV-990 No 30-5) *Span:* 36.58 m (120 ft) *Length:* 42.43 m (139 ft 2½ in) *Max take-off weight:* 114,760 kg (253,000 lb) *Powerplant:* 4 × General Electric CJ-805-23C turbofans, each 7,280 kg (16,050 lb) st *Max cruising speed:* 990 km/h (615 mph) *Range:* 6,115 km (3,800 miles) *Accommodation:* 106 passengers, 4 crew

de Havilland (BAe) Comet 4C
The first pure-jet airliner to go into service, the Comet first flew in 1949 and entered scheduled service with BOAC in May 1952. But early hopes were dashed by a disastrous series of crashes. The completely redesigned Comet 4 entered service in 1958, and although it was an excellent aircraft the initiative in jet airliner production

Comet 4C G-BDIW of Dan-Air landing at Gatwick. The last Dan-Air Comet flight was made in November 1980 (200 mm KR f4 1/500)

had passed meanwhile to the USA. (**Comet 4C**) *Span:* 35.05 m (115 ft) *Length:* 33.99 m (111 ft 6 in) *Max take-off weight:* 73,482 kg (162,000 lb) *Powerplant:* 4 × Rolls-Royce Avon 525 turbojets, each 4,763 kg (10,500 lb) st *Max cruising speed:* 861 km/h (535 mph) *Range:* 4,168 km (2,600 miles) *Accommodation:* 101

33

Boeing 727

The immensely successful Boeing 727 is the most widely used of all Western jet airliners, with production reaching well over 1,600 in 17 years to date. Outwardly similar to its design contemporary, the British Trident, the 727 is Boeing's only rear-engined production aircraft. Design studies for a short/medium-range jet to partner the four-engined long-haul 707 began in 1956. Production began in early 1963 and Eastern Airlines began scheduled operations in February 1964, with Lufthansa inaugurating European operations soon afterwards.

There were several accidents in the first year of operations, but improved landing technique overcame the problem and the 727 has sold steadily ever since. Boeing has undertaken continuous development: from the original 727-100 came the 100C Convertible freighter, the 100QC quick-change freighter, the stretched 200 series with seating for 189 passengers, and the Advanced 727 with quieter engines and improved weight and fuel capabilities. Plans for an even further stretched 727-300 series were abandoned in favour of developing the all-new 757.

The 727's good short-field performance results from a sophisticated wing incorporating advanced high-lift systems.

Left: Boeing 727 100C HI-312 Sandiez of Dominicana. Above: The 727 cockpit has a high degree of commonality with that of the 707. Right, clockwise from top: 727-200 Advanced EC-DDX of Iberia. 727-100C YA-FAU of Ariana Afghan Airlines. 727-200 I-DIRM of Alitalia. 727-100 N111EK of Mk II Leasing. 727-200 C-GAAI of Air Canada. 727-200 N412BN of Braniff Airways
Boeing 727

(Left: 300 mm KR f5.6 + ⅔ 1/500. Above: 20 mm KR f5.6 1/60. Right, clockwise from top: 300 mm KR f5.6 + ⅔ 1/500, 400 mm KR f5.6 + ⅔ 1/500, 105 mm KR f5.6 + ⅔ 1/500, 50 mm KM f5.6 + ⅓ 1/250, 105 mm KR f5.6 + ⅔ 1/500, 200 mm KR f5.6 + ⅔ 1/500)

Boeing 727-200 of Continental Airlines (300 mm KR f5.6 + ⅔ 1/500)

(Boeing 727-200 Advanced) *Span:* 32.92 m (108 ft) *Length:* 46.69 m (153 ft 2 in) *Max take-off weight:* 86,405 kg (190,500 lb) *Powerplant:* 3 × Pratt & Whitney JT8D-15, each 7,258 kg (16,000 lb) st *Max cruising speed:* 953 km/h (592 mph) *Range:* 2,970 km (1,845 miles) *Accommodation:* up to 189 passengers, 3 crew

British Airways Trident 3B G-AWZK on final approach to Heathrow at dusk (105 mm KR f2.5 1/125)

Hawker Siddeley (BAe) Trident
Commissioned by BEA in the late 1950s as a short-haul jet, the first flight was in January 1962 and airline service began in 1964. The original 1 and 1E versions were followed by the 2E with increased range and the 3 and 3B with a longer fuselage accommodating 180 passengers to the 2E's 132. (**Trident 3B**) *Span:* 29.87 m (98 ft) *Length:* 39.98 m (131 ft 2 in) *Max take-off weight:* 68,040 kg (150,000 lb) *Powerplant:* 3 × Rolls-Royce Spey turbofans, each 5,425 kg (11,960 lb) st, plus 1 × RR RB.162-86 booster turbojet *Max cruising speed:* 967 km/h (601 mph) *Range:* 1,761 km (1,094 miles) *Accommodation:* 180 passengers, 3 crew

Tupolev Tu-154

Tupolev Tu-154B P-551 of North Korean carrier Chosonminghang at Moscow's Sheremetyevo Airport (400 mm KR f5.6+⅓ 1/500)

Paralleling contemporary trends in the West, the designers of Tu-154 adopted the trijet T-tail layout of the Trident and Boeing 727. NATO code-named *Careless*, the Tu-154 has a six-wheel bogie main undercarriage which allows rough-field operations. First flight was in 1968 and development continues. (**Tu-154B**) *Span:* 37.55 m (123 ft 2½ in) *Length:* 47.9 m (157 ft 1¾ in) *Max take-off weight:* 96,000 kg (211,642 lb) *Powerplant:* 3 × Kuznetsov NK-8-2U turbofans, each 10,500 kg (23,148 lb) st *Max cruising speed:* 900 km/h (559 mph) *Range:* 2,750 km (1,708 miles) *Accommodation:* 169 passengers, 3/4 crew

Tu-134A YU-AJW of Yugoslav charter operator Aviogenex (400 mm KR f5.6 + ⅓ 1/500)

Tupolev Tu-134

The Tupolev Tu-134 short-haul airliner (*Crusty*) retained many features, including the wings and undercarriage, of the Tu-124, the aircraft it was designed to replace. The first flight was in 1963 and the type entered full service with Aeroflot in 1967, giving the Soviet carrier an aircraft matching Western standards of passenger comfort and operating economics. (**Tu-134A**) *Span:* 29.01 m (95 ft 2 in) *Length:* 37.05 m (121 ft 6½ in) *Max take-off weight:* 47,000 kg (103,616 lb) *Powerplant:* 2 × Soloviev D-30-2 turbofans, each 6,800 kg (14,991 lb) st *Max cruising speed:* 885 km/h (550 mph) *Range:* 2,000 km (1,243 miles) *Accommodation:* 80, 3 crew

McDonnell Douglas DC-9 Series 30

Responsiveness to customer requirements and a very high degree of "stretchability" in the original design have been the keys to the commercial success of the DC-9. In 1966, in response to an airline request, McDonnell Douglas flew the first 115-seat Series 30, with a fuselage stretched by 4,57 m (15 ft) – (DC-9-30) *Span:* 28.47 m

McDonnell-Douglas DC-9-31 of Hughes Airwest. This aircraft first flew with Hawaiian Airways (300 mm KR f8 1/500)

(93 ft 5 in) *Length:* 36.37 m (119 ft 3½ in) *Max take-off weight:* 54,885 kg (121,000 lb) *Powerplant:* 2 × Pratt & Whitney JT8D turbofans, each 6,350 kg (14,000 lb) st *Max cruising speed:* 907 km/h (564 mph) *Range:* 3,095 km (1923 miles) *Accommodation:* 115 passengers, 2 crew

McDonnell-Douglas DC-9 Series 40
The Series 40 stretched the original DC-9 airframe even further, offering an additional 1.88 m (6ft 2in) over the Series 30. the type offers high capacity over short ranges, making it suitable for high-traffic domestic routes. *Span:* 28.47 m (93 ft 5 in) *Length:* 38.47 m (125 ft 6 in) *Max take-off weight:* 51,710 kg (113,762 lb) *Power-*

McDonnell-Douglas DC-9-41 JA8442 of Toa Domestic Airlines, Japan's internal airline, at Misawa Airport (200 mm KR f5.6 + ⅓ 1/500)
plant: 2 × Pratt & Whitney JT8D-9 turbofans, each 7,010 kg (15,422 lb) st *Max cruising speed:* 903 km/h 561 mph) *Range:* 1,078 km (670 miles) *Accommodation:* 132 passengers, 2 crew

McDonnell-Douglas DC-9 Series 50
Approaching the ultimate in stretch, the DC-9-50 marries the Series 30 wing with a fuselage nearly 30% longer than that of the original Series 10. Swissair originated the requirement and put the model into service in 1975. The same airline has ordered the DC-9 Super 80, which features even greater stretch and capacity for

DC-9-51 of Swissair, the airline which first ordered the type (200 mm KR 5.6 + ⅓ 1/500)

172 passengers. *Span:* 28.47 m (93 ft 5 in) *Length:* 40.72 m (133 ft 7¾ in) *Max take-off weight:* 54,885 kg (121,000 lb) *Powerplant:* 2 × Pratt & Whitney JT8D-17 turbofans, each 7,258 kg (16,000 lb) st *Max cruising speed:* 929 km/h (577 mph) *Range:* 2,390 km (1,485 miles) *Accommodation:* 139, 2 crew

Fokker F.28 Fellowship Mk 1000
Designed as a pure-jet successor to the successful twin-turboprop F.27, the F.28
short-haul feederliner was funded by an international consortium which included
Shorts, VFW-Fokker and MBB. The type first flew in 1967 and has sold steadily
since then in six different models, the Mk 6000 carrying up to 85 passengers. A

Air Alpes F.28 Mk 1000 F-BUTI at Le Bourget (105 mm KR f5.6 + ⅔ 1/500)
convertible freight model is available. (**F.28 Mk 1000**) *Span:* 23.58 m (77 ft 4¼ in)
Length: 27.4 m (89 ft 10¾ in) *Powerplant:* 2 × Rolls-Royce RB.183 2 Spey turbofans, each 4,468 kg (9,850 lb) st *Max cruising speed:* 843 km/h (524 mph) *Range:*
1,705 km (1,059 miles) *Accommodation:* up to 65 passengers, 2/3 crew

43

Boeing 737-200 N23SW of Southwest Airlines at Harlingen, Texas (300 mm KR f8 1/500)

Boeing 737

Boeing came late to the short-haul twinjet market, but since its first flight in 1967 the 737 has enjoyed great success. Although a completely new design, the 737 shares important design and component features with the 707 and 727. Airline service began with Lufthansa's 737-100 1n 1967, but the biggest-selling version has been the 737-200 with a stretched fuselage and high-density seating for 130. This model is available in convertible freight/passenger form and as the Advanced 737-200 with

Boeing 737-200 7T-VEF Sauoara of Air Algérie approaches Heathrow (300 mm KR f5.6 + ⅓ 1/500)

many detail improvements. Although the type is well proven as a short/medium-range transport, Boeing has proposed a long-range Advanced 737-200 with extra fuel and uprated engines. Meanwhile, the original aircraft continues in production in response to orders from major operators. (**Boeing 737-200**) *Span:* 28.3 m (93 ft)

Length: 30.48 (100 ft) *Powerplant:* 2 × Pratt & Whitney JT8D-17 turbofans, each 7,258 kg (16,000 lb) st *Max cruising speed:* 908 km/h (564 mph) *Range:* 2,817 km (1,750 miles) *Accommodation:* 130, 2 crew

BAC (BAe) One-Eleven

First flown in 1963, the BAC One-Eleven short/medium-range jet transport is still in production under licence in Romania and remains Britain's most commercially successful jet airliner. British United Airways and Braniff in the USA began scheduled operations with the Series 200 in 1965. Since then the type has been

BAC One-Eleven Series 516FP TG-AZA of Aviateca Aerolineas de Guatemala (105 mm KR f5.6 + ⅔ 1/500)

developed through the Series 300, 400, 475 and the long-fuselage Series 500 (**Srs. 500**) *Span:* 28.5 m (93 ft 6 in) *Length:* 32.61 m (107 ft) *Powerplant:* 2 × Rolls-Royce RB.163 Spey turbofans, each 5,693 kg (12,550 lb) st *Max cruising speed:* 871 km/h (541 mph) *Range:* 2,744 km (1,705 miles) *Accommodation:* 119, 2 crew

Dassault-Breguet Mercure F-BTTB of Air Inter at the 1975 Paris Show (105 mm KII f5.6 + ⅓ 1/250)

Dassault-Breguet Mercure

A brave attempt by Dassault to produce a private-venture European short-haul airliner, the Mercure failed to fulfil its initial promise and only two prototypes and ten production aircraft were built. The first prototype flight was in 1971 and scheduled services with French domestic operator Air Inter began in 1974. (**Mercure**) *Span:* 30.55 m (100 ft 3 in) *Length:* 34.84 m (114 ft 3½ in) *Powerplant:* 2 × Pratt & Whitney JT8D-15 turbofans, each 7,031 kg (15,500 lb) st *Max cruising speed:* 925 km/h (575 mph) *Range:* 2,085 km (1,296 miles) *Accommodation:* up to 162 passengers, 2 crew

VFW 614
Planned in the mid-1960s as a DC-3 replacement, the prototype VFW 614 flew in 1971, with production deliveries beginning in 1975. The unusual above-wing engine location offered several design advantages, but the short-haul feederliner failed to win any major orders and plans for a stretched development and further production

VFW 614 F-GATG of French domestic operator Air Alsace (200 mm KR f8 1/500) were abandoned after 16 aircraft had been completed. (**VFW 614-100**) *Span:* 21.5 m (70 ft 6½ in) *Length:* 20.6 m (67 ft 7 in) *Powerplant:* 2 × Rolls-Royce M45H turbofans, each 3,302 kg (7,280 lb) st *Max cruising speed:* 705 km/h (438 mph) *Range:* 1,205 km (749 miles) *Accommodation:* 44 passengers, 2 crew

Sud Aviation (Aérospatiale) Caravelle

A true signpost in post-war aviation, the graceful Caravelle was the world's first short-haul jet airliner and the first to be powered by rear-mounted engines. The first flight was in 1955 but airline service with Air France did not begin until 1959. Developed through several versions and sold and operated widely around the world,

Caravelle Series III F-BNKA of Air Inter (200 mm KR f4.5 1/500)
the Caravelle remained in production until 1972. (**Caravelle Series III**) *Span:* 34.3 m (112 ft 6 in) *Length:* 32.01 m (105 ft) *Powerplant:* 2 × Rolls-Royce Avon 527 turbojects, each 4,763 kg (11,400 lb) st *Max cruising speed:* 805 km/h (500 mph) *Range:* 1,700 km (1,056 miles) *Accommodation:* 80 passengers, 2/3

49

Tupolev Tu-104
The Soviet Union's veteran jet airliner, the Tu-104 was based on the Tu-16 strategic bomber and first flew in 1955. Early versions carried 48 passengers over short/medium ranges in somewhat primitive conditions, but the type was improved through the 70-seat Tu-104A and the 100-seat Tu-104B. Production ended in 1960

Tu-104A CCCP-42456 of Aeroflot at Moscow's Sheremetyevo Airport (400 mm KR f5.6 + ⅓ 1/500) after more than 200 had been built. NATO code name *Cookpot*. (**Tu-104A**) *Span:* 34.54 m (113 ft 4 in) *Length:* 38.85 m (127 ft 5½ in) *Powerplant:* 2 × Mikulin AM-3 turbojets, each 8,700 kg (19,180 lb) st *Max cruising speed:* 900 km/h (559 mph) *Range:* 2,650 km (1,647 miles) *Accommodation:* 70 passengers, 3/4 crew

Antonov An-72
Still very much a research programme, the An-72 was developed in response to an Aeroflot request for a civil STOL transport, though it will undoubtedly have military applications. The twin turbofans exhaust above the "blown" wing, which, with its flaps and spoilers, generates a great deal of lift. (**An-72**) *Span:* 25.83 m (84 ft 9 in)

An-72 CCCP-83966 in Aeroflot markings at the 1979 Paris Show (50 mm KM f5.6+⅓ 1/250)
Length: 26.58 m (87 ft 2¾ in) *Powerplant:* 2 × Lotarev D-36 turbofans, each 6,485 kg (114,297 lb) st *Max cruising speed:* 720 km/h (447 mph) *Range:* 1,000 km (621 miles) *Accommodation:* 7,500 kg (16,535 lb) freight, up to 52 passengers, 3 crew

Yakovlev Yak-40
First flown in 1966, the Yak-40 went into large-scale production a year later and is now widely used within the Soviet Union. It is typical of Soviet aircraft in being able to operate autonomously from short, rugged airfields. The Yak-40, NATO code-named *Codling*, has undergone modification and improvement in service, and a cargo

Yakovlev Yak-40 OK-FEI of CSA at Prague Airport (400 mm KR f5.6 + ⅓ 1/500) version with a large loading door on the port side has been built. (**Yak-40**) *Span:* 25 m (82 ft 0¼ in) *Length:* 20.36 m (66 ft 9½ in) *Powerplant:* 3 × Ivchenko AI-25 turbofans, each 1,500 kg (3,307 lb) st *Max cruising speed:* 550 km/h (342 mph) *Range:* 1,450 km (901 miles) *Accommodation:* 33 passengers, 2/3 crew

Yakovlev Yak-42
A follow-on from the Yak-40, the Yak-42, NATO code-named *Clobber*, is a much larger, more ambitious and advanced airliner designed to replace the 1960s generation of Soviet aircraft over short and medium ranges. While incorporating sophisticated technology, the aircraft still displays typical ruggedness and on-board auxili-

Yakovlev Yak-42 CCCP-42304 in Aeroflot markings at the 1979 Paris Show (50 mm KM f5.6 + ⅓ 1/250) ary power and handling equipment. (**Yak-42**) *Span:* 34.2 m (112 ft 2½ in) *Length:* 36.38 m (119 ft 4½ in) *Powerplant:* 3 × Lotarev D-36 turbofans, each 6,485 kg (14,297 lb) st *Max cruising speed:* 820 km/h (510 mph) *Range:* 1,000 km (621 miles) *Accommodation:* 120, 2 crew

53

Canadair CL-600 Challenger
Designed for the top end of the executive jet market, the CL-600, with its spacious cabin accommodating 30 passengers, could also be a useful short-haul commuter airliner or express cargo aircraft. The prototype, based on the LearStar 600, first flew in 1978. (**CL-600**) *Span:* 18.83 m (61 ft 10 in) *Length:* 20.82 m (68 ft 5 in) *Power-*

Canadair Challenger prototype C-GCGS-X at the 1979 Paris Show (300 mm KR f5.6 + ⅓ 1/500) plant: 2 × ALF502 turbofans, each 2,950 kg (6,500 lb) st *Max cruising speed:* 935 km/h (580 mph) *Range:* 8,425 km (5,120 miles) *Accommodation:* 30 passengers, 2 crew

Gulfstream American (Grumman) Gulfstream II
A large executive transport, the Gulfstream II is also operated by charter companies or as a VIP transport. First flight was in October 1966 and 256 were built before production ended in 1979. The Gulfstream III has a redesigned wing and extended fuselage. (**Gulfstream II**) *Span:* 20.98 m (68 ft 10 in) *Length:* 24.36 m (79 ft 11 in)

Gulfstream II HZ-AFI, used by Saudia as a VIP transport (105 mm KM f5.6 + ⅓ 1/250)
Max take-off weight: 29,711 kg (65,500 lb) *Powerplant:* 2 × Rolls-Royce Spey turbofans, each 5,170 kg (11,400 lb) st *Max cruising speed:* 936 km(h (581 mph) *Range:* 6,025 km (3,744 miles) *Accommodation:* 19 passengers, 3 crew

55

Antonov An-12

Originally produced as a military transport, the An-12 has an upswept tail incorporating a loading ramp and can operate from rough fields. First flight was in 1959 and since then more than 900 have been built, some 200 serving with Aeroflot as cargo/passenger transports. (**An-12**) *Span:* 38.00 m (124 ft 8 in) *Length:* 33.00 m

An-12 CCCP-11105 of Aeroflot (200 mm KM f8 1/125)
(108 ft 3 in) *Max take-off weight:* 61,000 kg (134 ,480 lb) *Powerplant:* 4 × Ivchenko AI-20K turboprops, each 4,000 ehp *Max cruising speed:* 600 km/h (373 mph) *Range:* 3,400 km (2,110 miles) *Accommodation:* 14 passengers/freight, 5 crew

Lockheed L-100 Hercules
The first civil Hercules flew in 1964, the type having already proven itself as a military freighter. The L-100-20 featured a stretched fuselage and the further refined -30 saw the elimination of some superfluous military features. The first L-100-30 flew in December 1970. (**L-100-30**) *Span:* 40.41 m (132 ft 7 in) *Length:* 34.37 m (112 ft

Lockheed L-100-30 Hercules N18ST of Transinternational (200 mm KR f5.6 + ⅓ 1/500) 9 in) *Max take-off weight:* 70,308 kg (155,000 lb) *Powerplant:* 4 × Allison 501 -D22A turboprops, each 4,508 ehp *Max cruising speed:* 581 km/h (361 mph) *Range:* 3,363 km (2,090 miles) *Accommodation:* 23,137 kg (51,007 lb) cargo/105 passengers, 4/5 crew

Lockheed Electra L-188

Developed in response to the success of the British Vickers Viscount in the early 1950s, the L-188 was America's only large turboprop airliner. Its early career was marred by a series of crashes which put a stop to further sales. Redesign of the engine mountings solved the problem and the type provided the basis of the

Lockheed Electra L-188C N171PS of Pacific Southwest Airlines (200 mm KR f5.6+⅔ 1/500) long-serving P-3 Orion martitime patrol aircraft. (**L-188C**) *Span:* 30.18 m (99 ft) *Length:* 31.9 m (104 ft 8 in) *Max take-off weight:* 52,617 kg (116,000 lb) *Power-plant:* 4 × Allison 501-D13 turboprops, each 3,750 ehp *Max cruising speed:* 652 km/h (405 mph) *Range:* 4,023 km (2,500 miles) *Accommodation:* 99, 3/4 crew

Ilyushin Il-18
Following a first flight in 1957, the Il-18 soon proved itself as a successful medium-range airliner and was developed through several variants and widely exported. The Il-18V had seating increased to 111 and the Il-18D had increased range and could seat up to 125 passengers. The medium-range Il-18E is the definitive model, with

Il-18V of CSA OK-PAG at Prague Airport (400 mm KR f5.6 + ⅓ 1/500)
convertible seating layouts. (**Il-18E**) *Span:* 37.4 m (122 ft 8 in) *Length:* 35.9 m (117 ft 9 in) *Max take-off weight:* 61,200 kg (134,920 lb) *Powerplant:* 4 × Ivchenko AI-20M turboprops, each 4,250 ehp *Max cruising speed:* 650 km/h (404 mph) *Range:* 2,500 km (1,553 miles) *Accommodation:* 122 passengers, 4/5 crew

Aero Spacelines Guppy

The first of the extraordinary "Pregnant Guppy" outsize freighters, converted from the old Boeing 377s, first flew in 1962. One of their newest tasks is the support of the European Airbus programme, and the turboprop-powered Guppy 201 ferries A300 subassemblies to the final assembly plant at Toulouse. **(Guppy 201)** *Span:* 47.62 m

Super Guppy 201 F-BPPA, operated by Aéromaritime in support of the A300 programme (105 mm KM f5.6 + ⅓ 1/250)
(156 ft 3 in) *Length:* 43.84 m (143 ft 10 in) *Max take-off weight:* 77,111 kg (170,000 lb) *Powerplant:* 4 × Allison 501-D22C, each 4,912 ehp *Max cruising speed:* 463 km/h (288 mph) *Range:* 813 km (505 miles) *Accommodation:* 24,494 kg (53,000 lb) cargo, 3/4 crew

de Havilland Canada DHC-7 Dash 7

Combining the passenger comfort of a large airliner with outstanding STOL performance, the Dash-7 is also exceptionally quiet. Its take-off run of only 610 m (2,000 ft) should make it very attractive to short-haul inter-city operators. (**DHC-7**) *Span:* 28.35 m (93 ft) *Length:* 24.58 m (80 ft 7¾ in) *Max take-off weight:* 19,731 kg

de Havilland Canada's DHC-7 demonstrator, C-GNBX, at the 1979 Paris Show (300 mm KR f5.6 + ⅓ 1/500)

(43,500 lb) *Powerplant:* 4 × Pratt & Whitney PT6A-50 turboprops, each 1,120 ehp *Max cruising speed:* 426 km/h (265 mph) *Range:* 1,303 km (810 miles) *Accommodation:* 50 passengers, 3/4 crew

Vickers (BAe) Viscount   *Viscount 810 G-AZLT of British Midland Airways. This aircraft was originally delivered to South African Airways (200 mm KR f5.6 + ⅓ 1/500)*
The Viscount first flew in 1948 and inaugurated the world's first turboprop-powered
airline service in 1953. The first production version was the Series 700, seating 59
passengers. The Viscount has since been stretched through several variants, the
Series 800 seating up to 65 passengers. Over 440 of all variants were built.

(**Viscount Series 810**) *Span:* 28.56 m (93 ft 8½ in) *Length:* 26.11 m (85 ft 8 in) *Max take-off weight:* 32,886 kg (72,500 lb) *Powerplant:* 4 × Rolls-Royce Dart turbo-props, each 1,990 ehp *Max cruising speed:* 575 km/h (357 mph) *Range:* 2,554 km (1,587 miles) *Accommodation:* 65 passengers, 5 crew

Canadair CL-44

Based on the military CC-106 Yukon freighter (itself a development of the Bristol Britannia), the CL-44D-4 civil freighter first flew in 1960. The hinged rear fuselage and tail section allows direct bulk loading. The CL-44J model has a stretched fuselage. (**CL-44D-4**) *Span:* 43.37 m (142 ft 3½ in) *Length:* 41.73 m (136 ft 10¾ in)

Canadair CL-44D-2 G-AXUL of Transmeridian Air Cargo (200 mm KR f5.6 + ⅓ 1/500)
Max take-off weight: 95,256 kg (210,000 lb) *Powerplant:* Rolls-Royce Tyne Mk 515 turboprops, each 5,730 ehp *Max cruising speed:* 620 km/h (385 mph) *Range:* 5,246 km (3,260 miles) *Accommodation:* 29,995 kg (66,128 lb) cargo/178 passengers, 3 crew

63

Handley Page Herald

Designed in the early 1950s as a DC-3 replacement, the Herald first flew in 1955, powered by four piston engines. The initial production Series 100 had two Dart turboprops, and the Series 200 had a fuselage stretched to seat 56 passengers instead of 47. The Herald was overshadowed by the highly successful Fokker F.27

Handley Page Herald 200 G-BDZV in the markings of British Island Airways (now Air UK) (200 mm KR f5.6 + ⅓ 1/500) and only 48 were built. (**Herald HPR.7**) *Span:* 28.89 m (94 ft 9½ in) *Length:* 23.01 m (75 ft 6 in) *Max take-off weight:* 19,505 kg (43,000 lb) *Powerplant:* 2 × Rolls-Royce Dart 527 turboprops, each 2,105 ehp *Max cruising speed:* 435 km/h (270 mph) *Range:* 1,127 km (700 miles) *Accommodation:* 56 passengers, 2 crew

F.27 Mk 100 ZK-NAF of Air New Zealand takes off from Christchurch Airport (400 mm KR f5.6 + ⅓ 1/500)

Fokker F.27 Friendship

Orders for the F.27 short/medium-haul airliner have totalled over 680 since the prototype first flew in 1955 and it is still in production. The F.27 was built under licence in the USA by Fairchild as the FH-227. Variants are the Mks 100, 200, 300, 400/600 and the stretched-fuselage Mk 500. **(F-27 Mk 500)** *Span:* 29 m (92 ft 2 in)

Length: 25.06 m (82 ft 2½ in) *Max take-off weight:* 20,412 kg (45,000 lb) *Power-plant:* 2 × Rolls-Royce Dart 532-7R turboprops, each 2,140 ehp *Max cruising speed:* 480 km/h (298 mph) *Range:* 1,740 km (1,082 miles) *Accommodation:* 60 passengers, 2/3 crew

65

BAe Series 2 ZK-MCA of New Zealand's Mount Cook Airlines at Mount Cook Airport (500 mm KR f8 1/250)

BAe 748

First flown in 1960, the 748 was originally the Avro company's proposal for a DC-3 replacement. Over 330 have been built and the type is still in production as a short-haul civil airliner, military transport and maritime patrol aircraft. A large number of 748s have been built in India under licence. (**748 Series 20**) *Span:* 30.02 m (98 ft 6 in) *Length:* 20.42 m (67 ft) *Max take-off weight:* 21,092 kg (46,500 lb) *Power-plant:* 2 × Rolls-Royce Dart 534-2 turboprops, each 2,280 ehp *Max cruising speed:* 452 km/h (281 mph) *Range:* 1,360 km (846 miles) *Accommodation:* 58 passengers, 3 crew.

NAMC YS-11

Built specifically for service on Japan's domestic routes, the YS-11A first flew in 1962 and went into service in 1965. Some 174 have been built, of which 76 have been exported. The type has been developed through -100, -200, -300, the military/freight -400, -500 and -600 series. **(YS-11A-500)** *Span:* 32 m (105 ft) *Length:*

NAMC YS-11A-500 SX-BBG of Olympic Airways (300 mm KR f8 1/500)

26.3 m (86 ft 3½ in) *Max take-off weight:* 24,500 kg (54,013 lb) *Powerplant:* 2 × Rolls-Royce Dart Mk 542 turboprops each 3,060 elip *Max cruising speed:* 472 km/h (293 mph) *Range:* 346 km (215 miles) *Accommodation:* 64 passengers, 4 crew

Antonov An-32

A development of the An-26 but with engines of much greater power, the AN-32, NATO code-named *Cline*, has excellent airfield performance, particularly in hot-and-high conditions, and has on-board auxiliary power. The military version can carry 30 paratroops, and civil freight/passenger versions serve with Aeroflot.

An-32 CCCP-83966 in Aeroflot markings (300 mm KR f5.6 + ⅔ 1/500)

(An-32) *Span:* 29.2 m (95 ft 9½ in) *Length:* 23.8 m (78 ft 1 in) *Max take-off weight:* 26,000 kg (57,320 lb) *Powerplant:* 2 × Ivchenko AI-20M turboprops, each 5,110 ehp *Max cruising speed:* 510 km/h (317 mph) *Range:* 2,200 km (1,367 miles) *Accommodation:* 39 passengers, 5 crew

Antonov An-24

Production of this short-haul workhorse of the Eastern bloc has run to over 1,000 examples, civil and military, since the first flight in 1960. The first passenger models seated 44 passengers, compared with 52 four abreast for the An-24V Series II. The An-26 development has a rear loading ramp for cargo handling. (**An-24V Series II**)

An-24V Series II YR-AME of Romanian airline Transporturile Ae

Span: 29.2 m (95 ft 10 in) *Length:* 23.53 m (77 ft 2 in) *Max t* 21,000 kg (46,296 lb) *Powerplant:* 2 × Ivchenko AI-24A tur 2,550 ehp *Max cruising speed:* 450 km/h (280 mph) *Range:* 550 *Accommodation:* 52 passengers, 3/5 crew

Convair CV-580
Numbers of Convair's post-war twin piston-engined 240, 340 and 440 airliners were converted to turboprop power with Allison engines (CV-580) by Pacific Airmotive in 1960. Convair also carried out its own re-engining programme with Rolls-Royce Darts (CV-600/640) to give the short-haul aircraft a new lease of life. (**CV-580**) *Span:*

Convair CV-580 N73153 of Sierra Pacific Airlines (300 mm KR f8 1/500)

32.12 m (105 ft 4 in) *Length:* 24.84 m (81 ft 6 in) *Max take-off weight:* 26,372 kg (58,140 lb) *Powerplant:* 2 × Allison 501 turboprops, each 3,750 ehp *Max cruising speed:* 550 km/h (342 mph) *Range:* 4,611 km (2,865 miles) *Accommodation:* 56 passengers, 3/4 crew

Shorts 330 N332GW of GoldenWest, the Southern Californian commuter carrier (300 mm KR f8 1/500)

Shorts 330

Ungainly-looking but good at its job, the Shorts 330 commuter and utility transport has a square-section fuselage and long, narrow wing, like its smaller stablemate the Skyvan. The 330 can be used for mixed freight/passenger work and is operated by several US and Canadian airlines. (**330**) *Span:* 22.76 m (74 ft 8 in) *Length:* 17.69 m (58 ft 0½ in) *Max take-off weight:* 10,161 kg (22,400 lb) *Powerplant:* 2 × Pratt & Whitney PT6A-45A turboprops, each 1,156 ehp *Max cruising speed:* 365 km/h (227 mph) *Range:* 804 km (506 miles) *Accommodation:* 30 passengers, 3 crew

DHC-6 Series 300 Twin Otter JA8798 of Nihon Kinkyori Airways (300 mm KR f5.6 + ⅓ 1/500)

de Havilland Canada DHC-6 Twin Otter

The Twin Otter STOL light transport first flew in 1965. Its rugged simplicity and good airfield performance make it particularly useful in undeveloped areas. There is a twin-float version with a shorter nose. The type also serves with the Canadian Armed Forces. (**DHC-6 Series 300**) *Span:* 19.81 m (65 ft) *Length:* 15.77 m (51 ft 9 in) *Max take-off weight:* 5,670 kg (12,500 lb) *Powerplant:* 2 × Pratt & Whitney PT6A-27 turboprops, each 652 ehp *Max cruising speed:* 338 km/h (210 mph) *Range:* 1,278 km (794 miles) *Accommodation:* 20 passengers, 1/2 crew

Swearingen Metro II

The Metro commuter airliner first flew in 1970, followed by the improved Metro II in 1974. An executive 12/15-seater is designated Merlin IVA. The type has proved popular for short-haul domestic operations and is readily adaptable to specialist uses. (**SA-226 TC Metro II**) *Span:* 14.1 m (46 ft 3 in) *Length:* 18.1 m (59 ft 4¾ in)

Metro II N5336M of Southern California commuter airline Sun Aire Lines (300 mm KR f4.5 1/500)

Max take-off weight: 5,670 kg (12,500 lb) *Powerplant:* 2 × Garret AiResearch TPE331 turboprops, each 940 shp *Max cruising speed:* 473 km/h (294 mph) *Range:* 346 km (215 miles) *Accommodation:* 20 passengers, 2 crew

LET L-410 Turbolet
This Czech light transport first flew in 1969 and scheduled services with the L-410A began in 1971. Export versions have Canadian Pratt & Whitney engines. The L-410AF aerial survey version has a glazed nose and an on-board darkroom. **(L-410A)** *Span:* 17.48 m (57 ft 4¼ in) *Length:* 13.61 m (44 ft 7¾ in) *Max take-off*

LET-410A Turbolet demonstrator at the 1979 Paris Show (200 mm KR f5.6 1/500)

weight: 5,700 kg (12,566 lb) *Powerplant:* 2 × Pratt & Whitney PT6A-27 turboprops, each 715 ehp *Max cruising speed:* 370 km/h (230 mph) *Range:* 300 km (186 miles) *Accommodation:* 19 passengers, 1/2 crew

Embraer EMB-110 Bandeirante

The first EMB-110s were delivered to the Brazilian Air Force in 1973. Since then this Brazilian light transport has proved very successful in civil service as a commuter transport and has sold around the world. The aircraft is produced in twelve versions and performs a variety of civil and military roles, including aerial survey and execu-

Embraer EMB-110P2 G-BGYU, operated by Air UK (300 mm KR f8 1/500)

tive transport. (**EMB-110P2**) *Span:* 15.32 m (50 ft 3 in) *Length:* 15.08 m (49 ft 9 in) *Max take-off weight:* 5,670 kg (12,500 lb) *Powerplant:* 2 × Pratt & Whitney PT6A turboprops, each 750 shp *Max cruising speed:* 417 km/h (259 mph) *Range:* 1,900 km (1,180 miles) *Accommodation:* 21 passengers, 2 crew

Beechcraft 99 Airliner N204TC of Bar Harbor Airlines operating commuter services in Maine, USA (300 mm KR f5.6 + ⅔ 1/500)

Beech 99 Airliner
Derived from the Queen Air light transport, the B99 is a 15-seat commuter airliner or air taxi. It first flew in 1966 and is also available as an executive transport. A cargo door allows all-freight or freight/passenger operations. (**B99 Airliner**) *Span:* 14 m (45 ft 10½ in) *Length:* 13.89 m (45 ft 6¾ in) *Max take-off weight:* 4,944 kg (10,900 lb) *Powerplant:* 2 × Pratt & Whitney PT6A-27 turboprops, each 680 ehp *Max cruising speed:* 451 km/h (280 mph) *Range:* 853 km (530 miles) *Accommodation:* 15 passengers, 2 crew

N262A N420SA of Swift Aire, a Californian commuter and charter operator (200 mm KR f5.6 + ⅔ 1/500)

Nord (Aérospatiale) N262

Based on an earlier unpressurised piston-engined transport, the Super Broussard, the N262 light transport first flew in 1962. It has been produced in A, B, C and D (military) versions, the last two being known as the Frégate and using engines of increased power. N262s operate with several French and US commuter airlines.

(**N262A**) *Span:* 21.9 m (71 ft 10 in) *Length:* 19.28 m (63 ft 3 in) *Max take-off weight:* 10,600 kg (23,369 lb) *Powerplant:* 2 × Turboméca Bastan VIC turboprops, each 1,080 ehp *Max cruising speed:* 375 km/h (233 mph) *Range:* 975 km (606 miles) *Accommodation:* 29 passengers, 2 crew

BN-2A Mk III-2 JA6401 of the Japanese domestic airline Nihon Naigal Koku (105 mm KM f5.6 + ⅓ 1/250)

Britten-Norman Trislander BN2A

The BN-2A is a successful short haul commuter transport first flown in 1970 derived directly from the twin engined BN-2 Islander (opposite page), sharing more than 75 per cent of components. The third engine is mounted in the fin. The Mk III-2 has a long nose containing a baggage compartment. (**BN-2A Mk III-2**) *Span:* 16.5 m (53 ft) *Length:* 13.33 m (43 ft 9 in) *Max take-off weight:* 4,536 kg (10,000 lb) *Powerplant:* 3 × Lycoming 0-540-E4C5 piston engines, each 260 hp *Max cruising speed:* 267 km/h (166 mph) *Range:* 1,610 km (1,000 miles) *Accommodation:* 17 passengers, 2 crew

Britten-Norman Islander
First flown in 1965, production of this versatile light transport has continued since 1966 and the type has sold around the world. The manufacturers are now owned by the Swiss Pilatus company. Military variants are known as the Defender and Maritime Defender. (**BN-2A**) *Span:* 14.94 m (49 ft) *Length:* 10.86 m (35 ft 7¾ in)

BN-2A Islander C-GILS of the Canadian operator Flight Center (300 mm KR f5.6 + ⅓ 1/500)

Max take-off weight: 2,993 kg (6,600 lb) *Powerplant:* 2 × Lycoming 0-540-E4C5 piston engines each 260 hp *Max cruising speed:* 290 km/h (180 mph) *Range:* 1,136 km (706 miles) *Accommodation:* 9 passengers, 1 crew

Martin 4-0-4 N967M of one of the type's last operators, Marco Island Airways of Miami (400 mm KR f5.6 + ⅔ 1/500)

Martin 4-0-4

Based on the 2-0-2 of 1946, the 4-0-4 was a stretched pressurised version and entered service in 1951. One hundred and three were ordered and some remain in service in the US and South America. **(4-0-4)** *Span:* 28.42 m (93 ft 3 in) *Length:* 22.73 m (74 ft 7 in) *Max take-off weight:* 19,000 kg (43,650 lb) *Powerplant:*

2 × Pratt & Whitney R-2800-CB16 radials, each 2,400 hp *Max cruising speed:* 450 km/h (280 mph) *Range:* 4,160 km (2,600 miles) *Accommodation:* 40 passengers, 2/3 crew

Convair (General Dynamics) 440 Metropolitan
First of Convair's post war twins was the 40-seat 240 of 1947 and the type was developed through the stretched 44-seat 340 and the 52-seat 440. Versions were produced for the USAF and US Navy and many have been converted to turboprop power (see p 70). (**440**) *Span:* 32.12 m (105 ft 4 in) *Length:* 24.14 m (79 ft 2 in)

Convair 440 N446JM of Mackey International Airlines operating between Florida and the Bahamas (105 mm KR f5.6+⅔ 1/500)

Max take-off weight: 22,271 kg (49,100 lb) *Powerplant:* 2 × Pratt & Whitney R-2800-CB16 radials, each 2,500 hp *Max cruising speed:* 465 km/h (289 mph) *Range:* 2,092 km (1,300 miles) *Accommodation:* 52 passengers, 3/4 crew

81

Douglas DC-4
First flown in 1938, the first production civil DC-4s were impressed for war work and the type went into large scale production for the USAAF as the C-54 Skymaster military transport. Civil production resumed post war and many surplus C-54s were demilitarised for commercial use and some are still in service. (**DC-4**) *Span:* 35.81 m

DC-4 N12190 operated by Air America (200 mm KII f5.6 1/250)
(117 ft 6 in) *Length:* 28.63 m (93 ft 11 in) *Max take-off weight:* 33,112 kg (73,000 lb) *Powerplant:* 4 × Pratt & Whitney R-2000-2SD-13G radials, each 1,450 hp *Max cruising speed:* 365 km/h (227 mph) *Range:* 4,025 km (2,500 miles)

DC-6B F-GAPK water-bomber of the French Sécurité Civile service (200 mm KR f5.6 1/500)

Douglas DC-6

To rival Lockheed's Constellation, Douglas designed a stretched pressurised development of the DC-4 and the resulting DC-6 first flew in 1946. The DC-6A and DC-6B are freight and passenger versions with a fuselage extended by 1.52 m (5 ft). The type was in production until 1958 and 288 were built. (**DC-6B**) *Span:* 117 ft 6 in (35.81 m) *Length:* 32.51 m (106 ft 8 in) *Max take-off weight:* 48,530 kg (107,000 lb) *Powerplant:* 4 × Pratt & Whitney R-2800-CB-16 radials, each 2,400 hp *Max cruising speed:* 507 km/h (315 mph) *Range:* 4,815 km (3,005 miles) *Accommodation:* 11,142 kg (24,565 lb) freight, 108 passengers, 3 crew

83

Lockheed L-1040 Super Constellation
The original Constellation first flew in 1943 as a military transport and was improved through a number of variants in post war airline use. The Super Constellation entered airline service in 1951 and the last of the line, the definitive L-1649 Starliner, in 1953. The USAF and US Navy also operated the type. (**L1049**) *Span:* 37.5 m

Showing her age but still with all the grace of the last of the great piston-engined airliners, N1007C, a transport
Super Constellation (300 mm KR f5.6 + ⅓   1/500)
(123 ft) *Length:* 35.41 m (116 ft 2 in) *Max take-off weight:* 54,430 kg (119,750 lb) *Powerplant:* 4 × Pratt & Whitney R-3350-CA 1 radials, each 2,700 hp *Max cruising speed:* 504 km/h (313 mph) *Accommodation:* 95 passengers, 3 crew

C-46A HH-AHA freighter of Air Haiti (200 mm KR f5.6 + ⅓ 1/500)

Curtiss C-46 Commando
The C-46, based on the commercial CW-20 prototype, partnered the C-47 (military DC-3) as a World War 2 transport and many were sold to civil operators at the end of the war, and some still continue today in both military and civil service. A total of 3180 C-46s were built. (**C-46A**) *Span:* 32.92 m (108 ft) *Length:* 23.26 m (76 ft 4 in) *Max*

take-off weight: 25,400 kg (56,000 lb) *Powerplant:* 2 × Pratt & Whitney R-2800-51 radials, each 2,000 hp *Max cruising speed:* 301 km/h (187 mph) *Range:* 1,883 km (1,170 miles) *Accommodation:* 2,950 kg (6,490 lb) freight, 2 crew

Douglas DC-3

Probably the most significant transport aircraft of the century, the DC-3 was conceived originally as a "sleeper transport", an enlarged version of the successful DC-2, in response to a particular requirement of American Airlines. The DC-3/DST flew first in 1935 and was an immediate success but its real potential was shown by its sterling services in World War 2 as a military transport. The USAF designation was C-47 "Skytrain" and the RAF's "Dakota". Surplus C-47s converted to carry passengers got post-war civil war transport off the ground again and many still soldier on around the world. There are many variants of the basic type and some have been fitted with turboprops. Over 13,000 were built including licence versions in Russia and Japan. (**DC-3C**) *Span:* 28.96 m (95 ft 0 in) *Length:* 19.63 m (64 ft 5 in) *Max take-off weight:* 12,701 kg (28,000 lb) *Powerplant:* Pratt & Whitney Twin Wasp radials, each 1,200 hp *Max cruising speed:* 274 km(h (170 mph) *Range:* 1,650 km (1,025 miles) *Accommodation:* 27 passengers, 3 crew

Left: C-47E N139D of Nevada Airlines. Above: cockpit of the oldest flying DC-3 Right: C-47B G-AMPO of the British operator Eastern Airways. Right below: DC-3 finished as the Douglas Company's 1935 demonstration aircraft (Left: 300 mm KR f5.6 + ⅓ 1/500. Above: 20 mm Speedlight KR f5.6 1/60. Right above: 200 mm KR f8 1/250. Below: 28 mm KM f8 1/125)

Canadair CL-215
The amphibian CL-215 is a purpose built "water-bomber", able to carry retardant or skim and scoop water from sea and lakes and dump it on forest fires. It has also been adapted as a search and rescue aircraft. (**CL-215**) *Span:* 28.6 m (93 ft 10 in)

CL-215 (F-ZBDD) forest-fire fighter of the Sécurité Civile of France (300 mm KR f5.6 + ⅓ 1/500)

Length: 19.82 m (65 ft 0½ in) *Max take-off weight:* 19,731 kg (43,500 lb) *Max cruising speed:* 291 km/h (181 mph) *Range:* 2,260 km (1,405 miles) *Accommodation:* 2,673 ltrs water/up to 19 passengers, 2 crew

Bristol 170 Freighter
Designed as a military transport during World War 2, the Bristol 170 Freighter first flew at the end of the 1945 and although used as a military aircraft, has seen most service as a civil utility transport and car ferry with its nose doors swallowing bulky loads. The passenger version was originally known as the Wayfarer. (**Mk 31**) *Span:*

Bristol 170 Mk 31 ZK-CRM of the New Zealand airline Safe Air operating a flying freight shuttle between the North and South Islands (300 mm KR f5.6 1/500)

32.02 m (108 ft) *Length:* 20.83 m (68 ft 4 in) *Max take-off weight:* 19,958 kg (44,000 lb) *Powerplant:* 2 × Bristol Hercules 734 radials, each 2,000 hp *Max cruising speed:* 264 km/h (164 mph) *Range:* 1,320 km (820 miles) *Accommodation:* 4,255 kg (9,380 lb) freight, 2/3 crew

Grumman G-21

Grumman's eight-seat G-21 commercial amphibian first flew in 1937 and original examples are still in use around the world. Military production versions were known by the US Navy as the JRF 1 and by the RAF as the "Goose". Some have been converted with turboprop engines as the Turbo-Goose executive transport. (**G-21 A**)

Grumman G-21A ZK-ENY of the New Zealand operator Sea-Bee Air (105 mm KM f5.6 + ⅓ 1/250)

Span: 14.95 m (34 ft 1½ in) *Length:* 11.7 m (26 ft 8 in) *Max take-off weight:* 3,630 kg (8,000 lb) *Powerplant:* 2 × Pratt & Whitney R-985-SB2 radials, each 450 hp *Max cruising speed:* 307 km/h (191 mph) *Range:* 1,280 km (800 miles) *Accommodation:* 7, 1/2 crew

Ford 5-AT-B Tri-motor N76GC used by Scenic Airlines of Nevada for sight-seeing flights in the Grand Canyon (50 mm KM f8 1/125)

Ford 5-AT-B Tri-motor
A veteran of the 1920s still in occasional airline service, the first Ford 3-AT Tri-motor ''Tin Goose'' flew in 1926 and was developed through the larger 4-AT and 5-AT until production ended in 1933. The corrugated-metal skinned airframe is especially rugged and long-lived. (**5-AT-B**) *Span:* 23.75 m (77 ft 11 in) *Length:* 15.44 m (50 ft

8 in) *Max take-off weight:* 5,670 kg (12,500 lb) *Powerplant:* 3 × Pratt & Whitney Wasp radials each 420 hp *Max cruising speed:* 172 km/h (107 mph) *Range:* 800 km (620 miles) *Accommodation:* 15 passengers, 2 crew

Hints on Photographing Civil Aircraft

Why do I want to go on taking photographs of aircraft? My answer is simple – because I love aircraft. Anyone who feels the way I do and is a skilled photographer has a wonderful opportunity to capture the excitement and romance of aircraft and air travel.

It is my personal wish to photograph all the aircraft in the world. This may be an impossible dream but as far as military aircraft are concerned however there is a finite limit. As for civil aircraft there are perhaps 20,000 commercial aircraft operating around the world from supersonic transports to veteran World War 2 transports still flying freight services to remote destinations.

A keen professional aircraft photographer might soon get jaded with his subjects, however rare the type and colourful the operator's scheme, but the opportunities to express one's feelings are always infinitely various in terms of light, season and background. A good photograph in my definition therefore is one that expresses, shows and speaks most clearly your own feelings about the subject – in my case, aircraft.

Technically speaking the most important thing is to press the shutter button at the best moment. With a dynamic subject like aircraft this may take time to get right but it should become intuitive with practice. A motor-drive certainly helps.

The most suitable camera is a 35 mm single lens reflex with convertible lenses. Telephoto lenses are essential but your lenses will have to be appropriate for local conditions. Normally a 100–200-mm lens will be sufficient but a 300-mm lens will cover long distance work forced by particularly difficult locations.

Besides cameras and accessories an airband (VHF) radio set is useful, giving you an insight into arrival and departure times, and binoculars are another useful tool. A map of the airport and outlying areas (where you are quite likely to be), plus scheduled airline timetables, are more useful tools for getting good results.

To photograph aircraft you have to go to them, they are not going to come to you with any worthwhile results, and unless you are a professional, the opportunities for real close up or air to air work are going to be very limited. The obvious places to go and see aircraft are at the airports of the world, although the great air shows such as the biennial Paris and Farnborough Shows offer excellent opportunities to get really close to the subjects. Civil aircraft also often turn up at military air shows and tattoos.

The trouble with airports is that although they contain a lot of aircraft, getting near them can be very difficult. If you are up on a public observation deck the light can be against you. The subjects are likely to be static or surrounded by attendant airport service vehicles. The subjects may indeed be at too great a distance to get satisfactory results however good your equipment.

Without doubt the best course of action is to go round the perimeter fence of an airport until a good vantage point is found. The end of a major runway will be the likeliest optimum point as there will be no buildings or other obstacles and a landing aircraft if caught at the right moment will fill your viewfinder.

The great international airports of the world – Los Angeles, New York, London, Miami, Paris, Amsterdam, Hong Kong and so on – will have the widest selection of types and operators although facilities will vary. Each airport will have its own characteristics but good results can be had by creating contrast by shooting in different weather conditions, light and seasons.

The smaller airports of the world offer greater intimacy and a chance to photograph older types working out their last years with small airlines. The combination of a rare and historic aircraft and a colourful scheme often makes a fascinating picture. Where military aircraft operate from civil airfields then the photographer is likely to find certain restrictions.

As for recognising aircraft types, individual aircraft and airline colours schemes, the following books are recommended.

Jane's World Aircraft Recognition Handbook, Derek Wood

World Airline Fleets, Gunter Endres

Airliner Production List, Nigel Tomkins

Encyclopedia of Airline Colour Schemes, Ian Mackintosh

All are available from Jane's Publishing Company, 238 City Rd, London EC1V 2PU

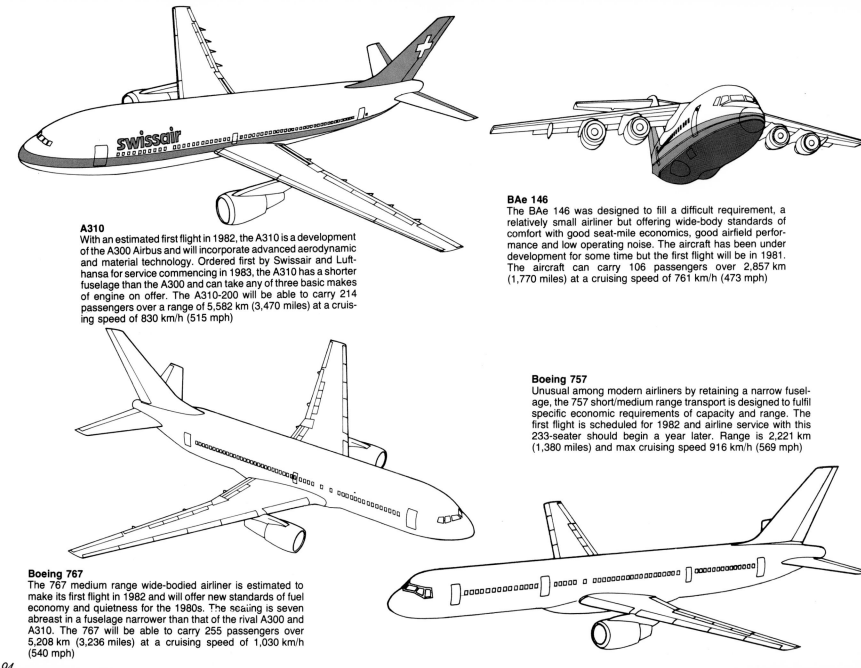

A310

With an estimated first flight in 1982, the A310 is a development of the A300 Airbus and will incorporate advanced aerodynamic and material technology. Ordered first by Swissair and Lufthansa for service commencing in 1983, the A310 has a shorter fuselage than the A300 and can take any of three basic makes of engine on offer. The A310-200 will be able to carry 214 passengers over a range of 5,582 km (3,470 miles) at a cruising speed of 830 km/h (515 mph)

BAe 146

The BAe 146 was designed to fill a difficult requirement, a relatively small airliner but offering wide-body standards of comfort with good seat-mile economics, good airfield performance and low operating noise. The aircraft has been under development for some time but the first flight will be in 1981. The aircraft can carry 106 passengers over 2,857 km (1,770 miles) at a cruising speed of 761 km/h (473 mph)

Boeing 757

Unusual among modern airliners by retaining a narrow fuselage, the 757 short/medium range transport is designed to fulfil specific economic requirements of capacity and range. The first flight is scheduled for 1982 and airline service with this 233-seater should begin a year later. Range is 2,221 km (1,380 miles) and max cruising speed 916 km/h (569 mph)

Boeing 767

The 767 medium range wide-bodied airliner is estimated to make its first flight in 1982 and will offer new standards of fuel economy and quietness for the 1980s. The seating is seven abreast in a fuselage narrower than that of the rival A300 and A310. The 767 will be able to carry 255 passengers over 5,208 km (3,236 miles) at a cruising speed of 1,030 km/h (540 mph)

INTERNATIONAL REGISTRATION MARKS

Arranged alphabetically in order of Nationality Marks

AN	Nicaragua	HMAY	Mongolia		
AP	Pakistan	HP	Panama		
A2	Botswana	HR	Honduras	TC	Turkey
A6	United Arab Emirates	HS	Thailand	TF	Iceland
A7	Qatar	HZ	Saudi Arabia	TG	Guatemala
A9C	Bahrain	H4	New Hebrides, Solomon	TI	Costa Rica
A40	Oman		Islands	TJ	Cameroun
				TL	Central African Empire
B	China	I	Italy	TN	Congo, People's Republic
C, CF	Canada			TR	Gabon
CC	Chile	JA	Japan	TS	Tunisia
CCCP	Union of Sovet Socialist	JY	Jordan	TT	Chad
	Republics	J5	Guiné-Bissau	TU	Ivory Coast
CN	Morocco			TY	Benin
CP	Bolivia	LN	Norway	TZ	Mali
(CR-C)	Cape Verde Republic	LQ, LV	Argentina		
CR, CS	Portugal	LX	Luxembourg	VH	Australia
(CU)	Cubana	LZ	Bulgaria	(VN)	Viet-Nam
CX	Uruguay			VP, VQ, VR	United Kingdom Colonies
C2	Nauru	(MONGOL)	Mongolia		and Protectorates
C5	The Gambia			VP-F	Falkland Islands
C6	Bahamas	N	United States of America	VP-H	Belize (British Honduras)
C9	Mozambique		and outlying Territories	VP-LAA to LIZ	Antigua/Barbuda
				VP-LKA to VP-LLZ	St. Kitts/Nevis/Anguilla
D	Germany, Federal Republic	OB	Peru	VP-LMA to VP-LUZ	Montserrat
DM	Germany, Democratic	OD	Lebanon	VP-LVA to VP-LZZ	Virgin Islands
	Republic	OE	Austria	(VP-PIA to VP-PZZ)	Gilbert Islands and Tuvalu
DQ	Fiji	OH	Finland	VP-V	St. Vincent and Grenadines
D2	Angola	OK	Czechoslovakia	VP-W, VP-Y	Rhodesia
D6	Comora, Republic of	OO	Belgium	VQ-G	Grenada
		OY	Denmark	VQ-H	St. Helena
EC	Spain			VQ-L	St. Lucia
EI, EJ	Ireland, Republic of	PH	Netherlands, Kingdom of	VR-B	Bermuda
EL	Liberia	PJ	Netherlands Antilles	VR-C	Cayman Islands
EP	Iran	PK	Indonesia	VR-G	Gibraltar
ET	Ethiopia	PP, PT	Brazil	VR-H	Hong Kong
		PZ	Surinam	VR-U	India
F	France, French Overseas	P2	Papua New Guinea		
	Departments & Territories			XA, XB, XC	Mexico
(F)	Djibouti	RDPL	Lao People's Democratic	XT	Upper Volta
			Republic	XU	Kampuchea
G	United Kingdom	RP	Philippines	XV	Viet-Nam
				XY, XZ	Burma
HA	Hungary	SE	Sweden		
HB + national emblem	Liechtenstein	SP	Poland	YA	Afghanistan
HB + national emblem	Switzerland	ST	Sudan	YI	Iraq
HC	Ecuador	SU	Egypt	YK	Syria
HH	Haiti	SX	Greece	YR	Romania
HI	Dominican Republic	S2, (S3)	Bangladesh	YS	El Salvador
HK	Colombia	S7	Seychelles	YU	Yugoslavia
HL	Korea, Republic of	S9	São Tomé and Principé	YV	Venezuela

ZA	Albania
ZK, ZL, ZM	New Zealand
ZP	Paraguay
ZS, ZT, ZU	South Africa
(ZS)	Transkei
3A	Monaco
3B	Mauritius
3C	Equatorial Guinea
3D	Swaziland
3X	Guinea, Republic of
4R	Sri Lanka
4W	Yemen, Arab Republic
4X	Israel
5A	Libya
5B	Cyprus
5H	Tanzania, United Republic
5N	Nigeria
5R	Madagascar
5T	Mauritania
5U	Niger
5V	Togo
5W	Western Samoa
5X	Uganda
5Y	Kenya
6O	Somalia
6V, 6W	Senegal
6Y	Jamaica
7O	Yemen, Democratic People's Republic of
7P	Lesotho
7Q-Y	Malawi
7T	Algeria
8P	Barbados
8Q	Maldives
8R	Guyana
9G	Ghana
9H	Malta
9J	Zambia
9K	Kuwait
9L	Sierra Leone
9M	Malaysia
9N	Nepal
9Q	Zaïre
9U	Burundi
9V	Singapore
9XR	Rwanda
9Y	Trinidad and Tobago